FROM EAST TO WEST:
A Young Man's Journey from Germany to America

―― *Peter K. Jentzsch* ――

www.ten16press.com - Waukesha, WI

From East to West: A Young Man's Journey from Germany to America
Copyrighted © 2022 Peter K. Jentzsch
ISBN 9781645383420
First Edition

From East to West: A Young Man's Journey from Germany to America
by Peter K. Jentzsch

All Rights Reserved. Written permission must be secured from the publisher to use or reproduce any part of this book, except for brief quotations in critical reviews or articles.

For information, please contact:

www.ten16press.com
Waukesha, WI

Edited by Jenna Zerbel
Cover design by Kaeley Dunteman

The author has made every effort to ensure that the information within this book was accurate at the time of publication. The author does not assume and hereby disclaims any liability to any party for any loss, damage, or disruption caused by errors or omissions, whether such errors or omissions result from accident, negligence, or any other cause.

Dedicated to all of my four children: Ulrich, Angelika, Silke and Olaf to share my life experiences; and to my dear wife, Sieglinde, who I lost in 2012.

. . . For as a ship sails beyond the horizon, you may not be able to see it any longer, but you know that it's there . . .

This work has been in progress since 2019.

FROM EAST TO WEST:
A Young Man's Journey from Germany to America

The way I came to America was from my mother's side. Edward Schulz (my maternal grandfather) had a windmill and later a "getreide muehle" (grain mill), powered by a waterwheel on a lake, creek, and stream. He had two brothers, Reinhold and Theodore. Reinhold went to America and settled in New Jersey. That was probably in the 1900s or so, and he started a regular sawmill and was successful.

The second brother, Theodore, went to the island of Rugen, the largest in Germany. He became a locomotive mechanic and driver of the island locomotive until he retired before the second World War. Over the years, the brothers stayed in touch.

I only remember my grandfather, Edward. I met him when he was already retired. His wife (my grandmother), passed on before him. They had five kids (four girls and one boy): Frieda, Else, Anna, Meta, and Carl was the youngest. Meta is my mother. My mother's sister, Frieda, was the oldest. She was eighteen years old when she got pregnant. Her boyfriend was the son of a doctor in Berlin. At that time in Europe, this was not socially accepted. The doctor's son could not marry a daughter whose father owned a mill, so the boyfriend's father talked to his son and said they would pay the girl a settlement!

She must have agreed to this, since they couldn't get married. At that stage, you could not see that she was pregnant. Frieda would not tell her father and mother that she was pregnant. That was a big shame at that time, so Frieda wrote a letter to her Uncle Reinhold in New Jersey which said something like, "I'm pregnant. My father should not know about it." She asked him if she could come over and stay by him in the U.S. Of course, Uncle Reinhold agreed and said, "You come over. I will not tell anything about it to your parents. I will never tell my brother. That's just between us."

Frieda then bought a ticket and came to the United States by steamship, and she lived here with Uncle Reinhold in New Jersey. Her parents never found out about her situation, but her brother and sisters knew about it. The cruise to America was on a steamship of the Hamburg-America Line. There were some people from Milwaukee onboard, heading back to the U.S. from vacation in Germany. A young man was there from Milwaukee by the name of Arnold Zeidelock, and his cousin, Henry Kretschma, was also there. Arnold met Frieda on the ship, and they fell in love. Arnold asked Frieda where she was going, and she told him that she was on her way to stay with her Uncle Reinhold in New Jersey.

Frieda told him that she was pregnant, the story of her lover and his father's involvement, and that she was going to have her child born in New Jersey. Arnold said, "It makes no difference.

I love you. I will come back to see you in New Jersey." So they exchanged addresses.

Frieda went to New Jersey. After a few months, Arnold came and met her in New Jersey. Uncle Reinhold was very protective of her. He said to Arnold, "Well, of course if you would like to marry her, you have my 'ok' to take her to Milwaukee, if that's what you have in mind." He said, "You better take care of her, because if you don't, I will come and get her." Arnold's parents were not happy about this; however, they tolerated their son's will.

So then Frieda moved to Milwaukee and got married. Her son, Curtis, was born in Milwaukee, and Arnold adopted him. Later, they had another daughter by the name of Ruth. As Ruth grew up, she went to college and became a medical technologist. She worked in a laboratory that checked blood samples. The firstborn child, Curtis, became a pilot and mechanic for Northwest Orient Airlines. His route with the airline flew from Minneapolis to Tokyo. He retired in about 1960.

When the children were young and in grade school, Frieda was homesick because she was the only one here in Milwaukee from her relatives, except for Uncle Reinhold in New Jersey. Her brother and sisters remained in Berlin. Her father was retired, and her mother had already passed away. Frieda wrote a letter to Germany and asked if anybody would like to come visit America. She said she was lonely and would like to have somebody here with her. She said it was not too bad over here, that she was happily married and had two children.

Her brother, Carl, he didn't want to follow in his father's

footsteps. My grandfather wanted him to get the mill and to take over the business, but Carl wasn't interested in it. He decided instead to go to Berlin and became a tailor, making custom-made suits. When Carl finished school, he said, "Well, I have nothing to lose. I'm single. I will go over to the U.S. and see Frieda." So he came over to the United States and settled in Milwaukee. Frieda was really happy when he came.

Then the depression came. Carl had a job in Milwaukee, but then he lost his job. It was a very tough time in America at that time. Carl had no money to go back to Germany, so he stayed here in Milwaukee. Frieda and Carl were happy in Milwaukee. They never went back to Germany to visit.

Carl married his wife, Irma, and they had two children, Beverly and Eric. Carl opened up a tailor shop and dry-cleaning business in Milwaukee, and he kept the business until he retired. The business's name was "World Cleaners & Tailors" on Kinnickinnic Avenue and Lincoln, on the south side of Milwaukee.

During the second World War, my mother and family lost contact with the family in the US. After the war, they got in contact again, but at that time we lived in the East Zone in East Germany, which was controlled by the Russians. My parents, Kurt and Meta, were divorced, and my dad lived in West Germany.

My father's family had no relatives in the U.S. He lived in the blue-collar district of Berlin. One day, my father recognized a man that was wanted by the police. He followed him until he met a policeman. He then told the policeman where the man was hiding. There was a reward offered from the newspaper publishing company for information to apprehend this man. The reward was given to my grandfather for his son. My grandfather convinced the fellow who was giving out the reward to give my father a job and schooling in the newspaper industry, instead of one thousand deutsche marks. They agreed on that.

I never met my grandparents on my father's side. My grandfather, Jentzsch, was a roofer at the Schultheiss Brewery in Berlin, a large brewery with several locations. He would do all of the roof maintenance. He lost his life early, through a work-related accident. My father was seventeen years old, and his sister was fifteen years old at the time.

My grandmother never remarried. She did get a lifelong pension from the brewery because of the accident. After the death of my grandfather, my dad was hired by the Ulstein-Verlag publisher. It was the largest publisher in Germany. After three years of schooling, he was a representative for advertising and marketing. He received the smallest territory and built it up. He did very good and was later promoted to a large, established territory.

An older colleague by the name of Ernst Goepfert retired, and my dad took over his customer accounts. They became close friends. Then my dad met my mother in Berlin at the KDW, short for Kaufhause des Westens. She worked for the Knorr Company and promoted Knorr Soups, etc.

Later, they got married, and I was born in 1935. Dad made very good money, and he purchased a car. We went on vacation in Bavaria and in Austria. I received three more brothers:

Dieter, Gunter, and Klaus. Then came the second World War. My dad had to leave his car in the garage (for gasoline savings). He used street cars, the U-Bahn (underground train), and the S-Bahn (city train). Taxis were also available.

The war went on, and the cities got bombed a lot. We had to go in the bunker. Later, we evacuated out of the city into Schlesia, which was two or three hundred miles out of Berlin. The school principal, the children, and my mother were with us. My dad was then drafted into the Army. He didn't like that, however, he served in the military in Berlin and the surrounding area.

One night, when he was home during an air raid, he went in the basement. He was knocked out for a while. When he woke up, he could only see dust from flashlight. That was the only time he used his gas mask. He went up the stairs to see the living area and looked at the stars. Everything was gone. At daytime, he found some pictures he could save in the yard. My mother received the news from my dad by mail.

The time was not good. My parents were getting divorced. My dad was in Berlin, and my mother was in Schlesia. The war came closer. The Red Army (Russian) came into Schlesia. We lived on a large corporation private farm (which produced sugar beets). The owner, Mrs. Rohjan, managed the corporation (her husband was in the war).

The day came when we had to leave, because the Russian troops were coming closer. Mrs. Rohjan organized the journey with our school principal (he was in charge of the evacuation of the children, etc.). The journey was by horses and buggies and a diesel tractor ("Lanz-Bulldog") with large air tires on the wagon.

The tractor pulled ten of us children, plus Mrs. Rohjan's two children. We left the corporation farm ("Das Gut") and went towards the city of Breslau (the largest city of Schlesia). It was a one-day trip. We drove at night so that the Russian air force wouldn't see us.

The tractor spit some sparks out of the exhaust pipe, and at night it was easy to see. We stopped as soon as we heard aircraft. Mrs. Rohjan's son was sick and passed away on the journey. The adults wrapped the child in a blanket and put him to rest in a ditch. There was not much time, the journey had to go on. Mrs. Rohjan must have been a strong woman.

We arrived in Breslau. The German troops kept the Soviets away from Breslau for this time. We slept on the railroad station floor for one night before we got in a freight car filled with straw, and the train took us to Berlin. The Red Cross fed us with milk, etc. It took longer to get to Berlin because of the Red Army (Russian troops). German military troops and sophisticated weapons were transported to the front to keep the Red Army away. Empty railcars were also used to transport civilians back to Berlin. We had to wait to catch an empty military train to go back to Berlin.

The train's purpose was to bring back weapons to the front, to Breslau. For sanitary purposes, a designated spot in the railcar was selected, and the waste was thrown out of the railcar in the countryside. These were tough times. My youngest brother, Klaus, stepped in a stone pot filled with syrup. I can't imagine what my mother went through. Our journey to get to Berlin took three days.

We came to Berlin, and my mother knew where her sister and husband lived at that time. The city was bombed out. We linked up with my mother's sister, Anna, in a small farm town called Karwe (near the city Neuruppin). The law in Hitler's regime was that farms had to take people in and give them shelter. They had relatively large homes at the farms.

We moved in at Duering's farmhouse and had two rooms and a kitchen. The war came closer. The "Himmler" artillery train with heavy weapons, waiting for the Soviet Troops, arrived across the Neuruppin Sea. Our mayor (Burgermeister) went to the commander of the Himmler train, asking them to have mercy on the towns because nothing would be left when the battle was over. The commander, soldiers, and train left our area. We heard that they moved the train to defend Berlin. Soldiers would throw chocolate to the kids out of the train when they moved. They knew that the war was coming to an end. The townspeople were relieved that the Himmler train commander relinquished the order to stay and battle.

On my tenth birthday, May 6th, 1945, the war ended. We saw the Soviet troops come in and ask for German soldiers, etc. We became under Russian rule. Our school became the Russian Kommandantur (Command station). We had school after two months, outside of the schoolhouse in the gymnasium.

After the war, Germany was divided by Russia, America, France, and England. We were not in the best section. Everything in the Russian Zone was communist and was very controlled. You could not write the truth in letters to relatives in the States because they always checked the mail. It was censored, especially if it was addressed to the United States or West Germany.

My mother, Meta, said my Uncle Carl knew that the situation in the Russian Zone was not the best. We received care packages from Carl and other relatives. He sewed the package together with linen and sent coffee, pepper, clothing, and other things. My mother would trade pepper to the farmers for meat at the time. The farmers needed pepper for sausage-making.

After a time, things began to get better. I was the oldest, and when I grew up, my mother said, "Well, you've all got to go to technical college and learn something." At Christmastime in 1945, after the war, my father visited us in the East section by Neuruppin. He lived in the American sector in West Berlin. My mother and dad had an argument about the gifts for us kids. In 1946, my parents got divorced. I was eleven years old, Dieter was nine, Guenter was seven, and Klaus was three. We would have liked for dad to be with us, instead of growing up without him. On top of that, because of the two Germany's (East and West), politics made things especially difficult. My mother, her sister Anna, and we four boys (Peter, Dieter, Gunter and Klaus) lived about one hundred kilometers away from Berlin. We lived in the country near the city of Neuruppin. We lived on a farm in a little town called Karwe. This is where we all grew up.

I was ten years old when the war ended in 1945. We lived on the farm and helped on the farm. We called the farmer "Uncle Duering" and became close friends! He was not our blood relative, but we lived there. My mother worked full-time at the farm.

When I finished grade school, I learned the tire trade. There were not too many trade colleges in 1950 to select, especially not in East Germany. I wanted to learn auto mechanics, but there were not enough automobiles being made, especially after the war, so I took the next best thing and learned the tire trade. I went to a technical college in East Berlin for three years. During those three years, each week I worked three days in the trade and three days in school.

During the trade school years, you don't make much money, but you made enough that you could buy cigarettes and beer, go to the movies and dancing. The company would pay for my train ticket to the school in Berlin. The school was free. After I got my diploma in 1953, I made good money, but only to East Zone standards (East German mark). In the tire trade, I worked with new tires and rethreading tires. That was the year of 1953. I was fifteen years old at the time.

In time, other opportunities came up! With education and trade experience, everybody can be retrained. Trade schools for construction, machinery, etc., were plentiful at this time (in 1952) with many new opportunities on the horizon. The Construction Union Berlin (Engineer Bauch was his name) and staff selected jobs for anyone who would like to change careers to make more money. New school and training were done.

I worked for the Construction Union Berlin. We built the jet airport for the Russian Air Force outside Berlin, right in the middle of the Schorfheide, formerly a hunting area, (Herman Goerings) in the woods. They took a lot of land out and made a big military airport. That was during 1951-1953 when the Cold

War was on, but that was the best paid job in East Germany (along with the steel manufacturing).

So we applied for that. We got hired, had additional schooling, and were retrained on equipment for special concrete runways, etc. Everybody was responsible for quality control on the job. The job was not boring, but fun. Everybody without technical trade college had a good paying job, as well as common labor for less money. To compare, my wages in the tire trade were DM 200 weekly net, and the construction union was DM 700 weekly net. Plus, we got DM 100 extra each month for being away from home.

We lived and stayed in barracks on the worksite for six days. Married men received DM 300 monthly and were away from the family. On the weekends they could go home. Living in East Germany, East Berlin, we can live okay if you stay in the East Zone! Apartment rent was not expensive. There was the construction kitchen menu at the worksite (not expensive), two menus only. A private, state-owned restaurant (Handel and Versorgung, "H-O" restaurants) were available on-site if wanted. Lots of selection for more money!

If you wanted to go to West Berlin, for one West German mark you had to pay 7 East German marks exchange. There was a big difference in bank exchange. We could not live in the West with that money, even though we made the most money in East Germany. However, in the West we couldn't compete. Our currency was not good.

When we went out, we saw the West boys. They had wheels. Some had cars and motorcycles already, and we had nothing to drive with. Anytime we wanted to dress ourselves in western clothing (which mostly came from the U.S., West Germany, and France), the clothing was in the modern style. It was hard to afford it. If we wanted to be in style, we purchased clothes in the West. For one pair of shoes, we paid almost 20 West German marks, seven times that much = DM 140 East German marks in 1953. However, we liked to impress the girls at dances with West-style living.

Me and my friend, Rudi Kaule, we worked for a while. We worked for a year and four months at the military airport for the Russians. Then we found out we didn't like that system anymore because it did not get politically better. We went to the West and saw the cars over there, the wheels and motorcycles, what the people all have, and there we had nothing to compare. We made good money for East standard, but that's all. We could eat. For fun, we had bicycles and girls, but that's all there was. Even the girls were not happy with the system.

So we decided to go over to West Berlin. There was no wall yet at this time. One day, we went over there to the West German police. It was a Friday night, Saturday morning, and we said that we didn't want to go back to East Germany. They allowed us to stay, like for others, in a refugee camp in Berlin.

We had to tell them what our last profession was, so we said that we had worked at the jet airport as construction workers, that we were familiar with airport construction for the Russian Air Force, and it was good news for them. We had to show the German police the latest layout from the airport. Then we also had to go to the Americans and to the English, all three of them, and had to show what new construction we put in, how thick the cement was, what the mixture was. We knew all that and told them and marked the new runways on the maps. At the English office, we got tea with milk. It was new for us.

Kaule and I were kept in separate rooms. The Germans told us that when we went to the U.S. people, they would offer us to go back to work on Monday. If we want to, we can get a little camera and take some pictures there. However, the German Police said they would not make us go. It's our free choice, but they would offer us that. They would drive us with a car to the border, and then we can go to work as we normally do. But if they (the East German police) ever catch us, they told us, "Then you guys know what will happen to you! If they catch you spying, you would go to Siberia," and that's it.

So we came in by the Americans, and what the German police had told us was true. The Americans were glad that we were there. We showed them all of the plans, the same as we did to the Germans. We couldn't believe they already knew where the barracks were at that time, where we slept, and how the airport was laid out. And then we added a lot of information they didn't have. They told us, "If you want to go back to work on Monday and take pictures, that would be better." Saturday came, and they gave us $20 U.S. a day. We had coffee, and they treated us very well. $20 U.S. x 4 West German marks = 80 West DM. 80 West DM x 7 East German DM = 560. Lots of money for us that day.

The U.S. offered (like the Germans told us), "If you want to go back, we will give you cameras and you can take pictures.

Then you can come back in about a week or whenever. If you ever come to the United States, you get five years free of tax." For five years of work, we would pay no tax. At that time, we never thought we would go to the United States. We were glad that we were in West Germany. It was great there, we were free!

Anyway, we said, "No, we will not do that." They said, "That's fine. No problem." Nobody made us do that, but they offered. Later on, I found out whoever did something for the federal government in that type of deal in the Cold War, these people didn't pay taxes for five years. When we came over to the U.S. later on, we had to pay taxes from the same day starting on when we came. In the States, we worked, and they deducted it like normal. That was okay. We never went back to the East to take pictures at the worksite. We only showed them what we knew. Besides, we didn't like the communist regime.

Then, after two weeks, we were flown out from West Berlin to West Germany, because you had to fly over the East Germany territory. Berlin was surrounded by the East Zone. It was all Russian territory, but the city was divided in four sections: American, French, English, and Russian. So we had to fly out from West Berlin. At that time, you could only fly Pan American or the French airline or the airline from England. Lufthansa couldn't fly there. That was forbidden by law. The four allies made the rule after the war.

Anyhow, we flew from Berlin into Hamburg. From Hamburg, they put us in a camp in Hamburg-Bergedorf. You could work in your trade or profession, if possible, doing whatever you like to do. The West German law and stipulation was that if a young person came from East Germany and they had no relatives in the West, first of all, they had to get on their feet again and make some money. You had to work for a farmer and make a contract with him for six months of work. Farmers needed help on the farms. All the money that you made went in the bank in a trust account, except for 10 marks weekly for pocket change. The farmer had to dress you and feed you and give you living quarters while you worked for him.

After six months, you received the savings and you were free to work anywhere. At least then you had money saved for renting an apartment, etc. You were independent and had a new start for the future. Wages were equal and paid promptly when the work time was served.

Regulations at the farm: holidays and weekends one day off, six months farm work. Most people had no relatives in West Germany. Jobs in their trades were not always available, and so they went to the farmers. The only way out of this strict regulation is if you have relatives in West Germany and they can get you a job and housing.

I had in mind I would call my dad. My dad lived in Hamburg. I found that out from my grandmother, his mom. My mother didn't want to give me my father's address, but she gave me my grandmother's address in West Berlin. That was when I was eighteen years old and worked at the jet airport in East Berlin.

I went to visit my grandmother before I came to Hamburg. My grandmother looked at me when I knocked on the door, and she said, "Who the heck are you?" And then she looked at me and said, "You must be Peter." And I said, "Yeah." She was so happy and cried. We did not see each other since 1944, before the second World War ended in 1945. My mother and us four boys were evacuated out of Berlin because of air raids. Grandma was retired in 1953, and I was eighteen. Grandma couldn't believe that I was here after all these years. We talked a lot, and she asked, "Where are the other ones?" I said, "My mother and the other three boys are still in the East Zone. I escaped, and I didn't go back." And she said, "My God, that's nice."

Then me and my friend (we call him "Kaule" because that is a short name for "buddy") went shopping with her, and she cooked for us. She said, "Next time you bring him along and I cook for you, and you guys can stay here for a couple of days," and we did. That was the time we came over to West Berlin. So anyway, she gave me my father's address and phone number. She said, "Your dad was here but flew back to Hamburg a week ago."

I contacted my dad before the youth farm program, and I said to him, "I want to come over to Hamburg if you can get a job for me." And he said, "What can you do?" I told him all of the things, and he said, "Yeah, you can get a job right away here, but I don't want you to come right away. You should work in the program with the farmer just like anybody else. There is no exception. This is a good program. I will not sign for it; however, I would like to see you here after the program."

I was kind of disappointed in him that he did not sign for my release. I didn't hear from him for a long time after my parents were divorced. The last time I saw him, I was eleven years old. In 1946, he came to visit us in the East Zone. There was no wall there yet. My mother and father had a big argument. The Christmas gifts he got for us were nice, however, we would have liked for our father to stay longer. He left the next day, and then I never saw him again until I came to Hamburg when I was nineteen years old.

Me and my buddy, we figured farming in the wintertime is the easiest, because then you don't have to be out in the field. You feed the cows, you do the machinery, refinish everything, paint, take the rust off, and grease everything. That's all done in the winter. And I said to my friend, "We've got to go around September," and we stayed and worked then. So we both did that.

There was an office that was in southern Germany, Mannheim. We had to go to that farm bureau office. We went and said, "We are here now and want to do our thing." We wanted to find work in our trade. Any time we came to an employment office in a new city, we showed our papers. They said, "Well, you guys never went to the farm yet?" We said, "Yes, we will do that sooner or later." But then they said to my buddy, "You better finish it and then be on to a new life!" So we did that and went to farm in the fall and the winter.

So that fella who was in charge of the program with the farmers, he had no car; he had a motorcycle. He took each of us separately to a different farm town. We were maybe twenty-five to thirty miles apart.

He picked out one farmer for me, and I came there, introduced myself. Then he showed me my room and the shower. There were two beds, and one student was there. He went to university for agriculture, and he lived in another town. His father told him, "You cannot stay on my farm. You go to another farm and work there." So he was there, and I worked with him, and we shared that room. On the weekends, we rotated the work, but we both had Saturday off.

Christmastime came and so on. I stayed with the farm family. They gave us all clothing. We had good food. They made alcohol in the wintertime. They had a lot of potatoes and had a regular distillery for booze. It was government controlled. You cannot get access to it. The alcohol goes into one big tank. Then, once a year in the spring, a wholesale distribution would pull it out, and they got good pay for it. It was good money, but he could not sell it to anybody. It was not like a bootlegger, but it was their biggest business in the winter.

I remember once I was sick and had the flu, and the owner said to me, "Come on in here, and I will give you a shot." He knew how to get one shot out, somehow. "You drink that, and then we have breakfast together in here and you'll be okay." And the next day I was okay, so it was a strong shot!

But anyway, when the six months were over, I got my check, and it was good. I had a lot of money saved that I earned for six months. They gave you interest for whatever came in, so that was good. I could live at least six months and get myself an apartment if I had to.

I had to look for a job. I went into the city of Mannheim and contacted my dad in Hamburg, and I had to rent a room or apartment. I had enough money to pay for my train ticket, etc. My friend left the same way, but he went to a different city. I went to Hamburg, but he went to Mannheim. He was an orthopedic shoemaker from trade, so he got a job there. I think he changed his job after a while and went to the chocolate factory. He met a girl there, and then he didn't like to go anywhere with me because he was settled with his girlfriend. But we stayed in contact.

So when I went to Hamburg at nineteen, my dad came and picked me up at the main railroad station. I came on the big train, and then we went on the city train. I went back and bought myself a ticket for the city train to go to his house.

So then he said, "You didn't have to buy a ticket. I already bought one for you." I didn't know that. He got a ticket for a whole month because when he was in business in Hamburg, he could take a train, the buses, the ship, the underground, and city train (S-Bahn). It was 24 marks for the whole month (parking was no problem). So when I found that out, I thought he was not that bad. First, I thought that he was stingy, but he wasn't.

I was nineteen when I saw my dad in Hamburg. My brother, Dieter, was seventeen years of age as he visited my dad. Third in line was my brother, Guenther, who came to the U.S. at seventeen years of age and joined the U.S. Army from 1962-1968. He visited our father in 1963 in Hamburg as a U.S. soldier. It was a great reunion for both of them. Guenther visited one last time in 1965. My youngest brother, Klaus, never met our father. He was fourteen when he arrived in the U.S.A.

So anyway, I got introduced to my dad's second wife, and we got along very well. They had no kids anymore. Our first Christmas came, and he told me he'd like to get a Christmas tree like we had when we were children at home. I contacted my friend, Rudi Kaule, and I said, "I'd like to go to Berlin and have Christmas and New Year's in Berlin," in the dance halls where we used to go, but in West Berlin. So my friend said, "Yes, I'd like to do that, too. We can meet in Berlin. I will fly from Mannheim to Berlin, and you can fly from Hamburg to West Berlin." And so I told my dad I would not be home that year for Christmas. It was not right. I know it now! And for my dad it was a disappointment, because after all these years I contacted him, but he didn't say anything.

Rudi and me stayed in Berlin, and we had a good time. We went by my father's sister. She lived in West Berlin. Her name was Walli, and she had one son, Gerhard, that moved to Canada. I don't know which province it was. I said, "Where is my cousin? Where is your son?" "Well, he went to Canada. He's been there already two years." I said, "Oh, my God. The time goes too fast." Then she said, "Would you like to read his letters?" And then she gave me all of his letters to read. And I said, "Yeah, that is really nice." He had some shoes there my size, and she said, "You can have them. He won't come back right now." So she gave me all kinds of shoes. They fit me perfect, so I didn't have to buy shoes for a while.

But then I had the urge to go to Canada, because I liked it when Gerhard said that it's different. When I came back to Hamburg after the holiday, I said to my friend, "Would you like to go to Canada? I think maybe we should go there and see my cousin. Would you like to come along?" "No," he said, "I don't." I said, "That's okay."

So I was living with my dad and working in Hamburg. I was still working in the tire trade. Then I said to my dad, "I'd like to go to Canada and see Gerhard, so that we can meet once." I remembered him before the second World War. He was five years older than me, and I thought that would be nice.

I wrote Gerhard, and he said, "Yeah, if you like to come, why not?" "The only thing is," he said, "you have to go through channels. You have to go through the Canadian Embassy, and you need a sponsor. Farmers will do this with a work contract for two years."

I went to the Canadian Embassy in Hamburg and put in for a visa. They said it would take probably a couple of months, but they would let me know. So I filled everything out. There was a question they asked about where you have your blood relatives. I said my father is in Hamburg and my mother is divorced from my dad. And, of course, I have three brothers, and they're all in the East Zone (the Russian Zone). They called it the "East Zone" at that time. I answered all the questions and hoped to get a visa and a sponsor.

After two months I got letter in the mail. I thought, "Boy, I got the okay to go to Canada." I opened it up, and it said they could not let me into Canada, and there was no explanation why. That was it. So I figure, "Well, what is the reason? Why did they do that?" So I went to the embassy myself, and I asked them, "What is the matter, why can't I get to Canada?" "Well, there's different reasons, and we won't discuss this now. That's the way it is." The meeting was done, and I was denied for no reason.

I went to talk to my dad about it. My dad worked for the newspaper all his life. He was in advertising. That was his profession, and he had a lot of ways to find out why I was denied. He went to the embassy and talked to them, and he said, "This is my son. He doesn't have any criminal record, at least not that I know of. My son grew up in East Germany, and he's now been in the West for three years living with me." He asked, "Why can he not go to Canada?"

They told him, "Mr. Jentzsch, you have an ex-wife in East Zone, plus you have three sons there, and the Canadian law is we don't let anybody in that has blood relatives in the East Zone." It was probably for political reasons, because the East Zone could put pressure on people. I imagine that they had reasons, so I couldn't go. I was really disappointed.

A year went by. I went back to Berlin once to my Aunt Walli, my father's sister. She was my meeting point in West Berlin. And I said to her that I need to write a letter to my mother. She needs to come to West Berlin for Easter. I want a meeting with her at my Aunt Walli's home. So she came. At that time, you could still travel between East and West Germany by train. Restrictions were not so tight yet that you could not travel. There was still no wall at this time.

My mother came, and my brother, Dieter, came along with her. He's the second oldest. The other two kids stayed with her sister, Anne, who lived with them in Karwe. I said to my mom, "How long would you like to stay in the East Zone yet? Right now, you can still walk over. Of course, you've got to leave everything there that you have, your furniture and everything. You can come as you are, but no suitcase because then they would be suspicious! But since you live there, it costs me the trip to Canada. That's why the Canadians won't let me in."

It was my wish to see Gerhard. That's why I talked to her that way, because she lived in the East Zone, and it wouldn't get better. "It will get worse, believe me." I said, "You should leave before anything else happens." But that was way before the Wall. Nobody talked about the Wall.

But my mother listened to me. She said, "Okay." This was before Easter. I hoped she would leave the East Zone. I said to her, "Do what you want to do." She went home, and they decided when Easter came along, they would leave the East Zone. I flew back to Hamburg.

My other brother, Guenther, was still in the third year of trade college. He maybe had one month to go, and then he would be done with his school. He had his diploma. Dieter is the second oldest and was done with his trade college. Klaus was my youngest brother and was still in grade school.

My mother had some friends in Karwe and thought they were nice. When she was in West Berlin, she bought books from the West. Everything was Western literature. There was nothing political in the book. They were regular books. She brought the books over to the East Zone, and when she read them all, she gave them away. You never throw anything away. And some people, they like to read them, too. But that was okay. They didn't say anything. My mom never told them that she planned to leave.

Easter came along. She did the spring cleaning: washed the

curtains, planted flowers, and decorated for Easter. We had geese and chickens. We had them all of the time for the eggs. And we had a little area where we kept the rabbits, and so she would feed the animals. Then in the morning, they left. They told these people a story that I was going to Canada and they'd like to say goodbye to me in Berlin, and so she spread that rumor. I did not know that she planned to leave on Easter. All her friends knew that I wanted to go to Canada. She said, "That's why we'd all like to go and say goodbye, because who knows when we will see him again." She made up that story.

I did send her a postcard from Hamburg saying, "Mutti, Happy Easter, Peter." So the postcard came, and the communist girl who lived in the same village (the girl mom always thought she could trust) read it. The girl said, "She told us they wanted to say goodbye in Berlin. However, Peter is in Hamburg. They've taken off." She alerted the authorities. I learned all of this after the Wall came down. We contacted friends where we used to live and found out that my mother's best friend, Mrs. Toppel, was the one who contacted the East-Volks police.

Naturally, they wanted to stop the train, but the train was already in Berlin. The first station was in West Berlin, and my mother, her sister (Anna), and my brothers were on the city train (S-Bahn) and left. In West Berlin, she got the first policeman she saw in the area. Usually, they have police patrol the borders between West and East Berlin. And she said, "We're here now. We won't go back." "Okay," he said. "No problem. It happens every day."

And then they said, "All right, we will put you in a refugee camp." So she went to a refugee camp in West Berlin for a while - not too long, maybe two or three weeks - and then they all flew out: my mother, my three brothers, and her sister. The West German government paid for their flight. You could not go by train or bus, because you would have to go through the East Zone. You have to figure, Berlin is right here in the middle, so everything around is East Zone. The only way to West Germany is to take a plane and go over. That's the way it was. There was a tremendous amount of money spent by the West German government to bring these people to West Germany.

So then they went to Hamburg, the second biggest city, and they had a big refugee camp in Bergerdorf. There were thousands of people there. There were big buildings erected there and divided walls with only curtains. Each one had rooms where you could sleep. The men and women were in separate rooms, except married couples. They had regular restrooms and showers.

The food was in a big, huge kitchen. The cooking was done by women employed by the government. It was all included, because these people had no money, so they stayed there and slept in their areas. It was pretty hard. My mother said there wasn't too much privacy, but everybody was adult. What could you do? That's the way everything was. The food and cooking were good.

Everybody stayed there until they were relocated into other cities, where they got jobs and started over. One family left at a time. That was all in West Germany where they put these people in different cities and different states. Germany has states, too. Not huge states like here. Bavaria is one of the biggest states there.

While they were in Bergedorf, my mom could write her brother and call the United States. She found out that her oldest sister, Frieda, had passed away. Frieda's daughter and son were still living, and they were already married. My Uncle Carl was married, too (my mother's brother). My mom told Carl the truth of how things really were in East Germany, how we had to leave everything there. My uncle said to her, "Get me a phone number for your camp there, and I will call you from the United States." More than once they talked.

But anyhow, my Uncle Carl told Anna and Meta that their sister, Else, was in West Berlin. She didn't lose her house in the war, so she was good off. He said, "Meta and Anna, you left everything over there. You've got to start new. Why don't you come over to the States, and I will sponsor you? If you have to start over, you might as well start here. At least we would all be together. We didn't see each other for thirty years." My mother agreed and said, "That's a good idea." She contacted the authorities in Germany, and she said, "Look, I've got a brother in the United States, and he would like that we come over there. If we have to start all over, then we might as well do that in the U.S."

At that time, my mother was fifty, my aunt was sixty, and there were my three brothers. My uncle said, "Okay, I sponsor you here in the States." And the sponsoring was like that. If you have people to sponsor, you have to have so much equity. Your house has to be worth so much, your shop, and whatever you have at the banks. If something happens to any of them in two years, or whatever it is, you'd be responsible for it. If they turn into criminals, it reflects on you. They had tough laws at that time. That was around 1956.

At that same time, in Hamburg, I switched from the tire trade. My dad took an extra distributorship on for a radio company they called Tefiphone. The first radios in the world came out with cassettes. You put them in, and there was music on it. You put them in the radio, and you selected as many songs as you want. You can reverse them and hear them again. That was a really big thing. The company originated in Cologne, and they needed distributors nationwide in Germany.

My dad said, "If you would like to go into sales, you'd be good in sales." Then he sent me to school, which he paid, and I did that while I worked. When he asked if I would like to come work with him, I agreed. I said I would love to go into sales. I'd make more money. I tried it for a few weeks, and I made more money on commission than I ever made working with the tires, so I figured that's the best way to do it, to go with him and do that.

We rented halls in hotels, and he advertised in the newspaper. And of course, he didn't give up his job as a rep of the newspaper. For promotions, we put big banners over the street. The TV foreign show was Friday, Saturday, and Sunday in that hotel, and we had a lot of people that bought them. A lot of sailors in Hamburg came in. They came here from the United States, Canada, and Australia, and we demonstrated the Tefiphone.

Hamburg is a big port town, and when these men came in with the ships, they had a whole three or four days off. They came to look at what's new. They found out about the Tefiphone and said, "Boy, we can buy these things if you can order them for 220 volts." 220 volt is European, 110 volt is American. We said, "Yes, it's available. We can do that, but that takes us longer." They said, "We're only here for three days in the harbor, but when we go out with the ship, in so many months we'll be back with a down payment. We'll take the order." We sold two or three of them. They must have sold them to friends overseas, because nothing like that was available at this time.

In the meantime, my Uncle Carl worked on the sponsorship. It takes about six to eight months, so I worked with my dad. Then I went by my mom and told her, "When Uncle Carl sponsors you, could he also sponsor me? If I couldn't go to Canada, I'd like to go to United States. Maybe it's just as good."

So then I wrote him personally, and I told him that I live by my dad, that I'm the oldest. He knew that my mother had four kids. He said, "Definitely, I will also sponsor you." So everything was in process, but nobody knew if this would go through or not. It was in the works.

Around this time, I told my dad several times I'd like to move out of his house where he lived. Grandma came from Berlin, sold her house, and she was living in Hamburg in his house, along with my dad and myself, so we had four people and a little doggie. That was okay, but I always slept in the kitchen at that time. They had the bed that was made like a couch. I'd come late at night, and in the morning I was gone already.

So I told Dad that I wanted to move out, but he reminded me that there were not enough rooms and apartments available. It was hard to find even one room. I said, "I know that, but I'm still looking."

When I worked with my dad selling radios, the radio business was very good. Whoever the dealer is, they are also responsible for the sale. The company would finance everything. If I sold a radio on a time payment (one year was the minimum), our commission was paid by the company. Now, the catch was if the deal went sour and the customer doesn't pay, you are responsible for getting that money. If you cannot collect the balance, they hold back from your reserve that was built up in your account.

Overall, we had no problems. But overseas buyers, they bought 110 volts. They'd pay cash at the time, and the radio went home on the ship and they sold them in the States or other countries. We didn't know what they got for it. We didn't care, because we got our money.

The domestic deals in Germany, I only had one who didn't pay, and that was a person who lived in a suburb outside of Hamburg. I had to go after the man. His name was Frickman. Since I had to chase him, the company told me there is no payment in that month, so I went right away to see what happened.

I chased Frickman to the house where he lived. A lady was at the door, and I said, "I'd like to talk to Mr. Frickman." Well, she said, "I'm sorry, he's out. We chased him out. He didn't pay the rent, and he's out of the apartment." I said, "But he didn't pay for the radio. I sold him a radio." I introduced myself to her and gave her my business card. She said, "You know what? Next to my house, his fiancée is living. If you go there, maybe she has the radio." So I said, "Thank you. That's nice of you."

Then she said by Monday she needed to rent a room. She was putting an ad in the paper, and by Monday the room would be available. I listened, but at first what I had in mind was to get the radio. I went next door, rang the bell, and the fiancée was there. I said, "Do you have the radio from your fiancé?" She said, "I have it, and I like it." And I said, "I have to get the radio back because the contract said he didn't pay for it. Unless you'd like to pay for it, then we can rewrite the contract, and you make the payments." The deal was made.

So I sold it to her, and she paid the monthly payment in the next three months. After that was done, I went over right away to the other lady and said, "I'd like to see the apartment that you want to rent." It turns out, it was the biggest room there with nice furniture. There was a bed, two chairs, a table, a restroom, and a shower was upstairs.

The landlord, Mrs. Milow, asked me if I'd like to get breakfast. I could have the room with breakfast or without breakfast. I said, "I like to sleep longer on the weekend, so I can do my own breakfast." She said, "That's fine. If you change your mind, let me know." So I right away paid 10 or 15 marks, and I said, "The room is sold. You don't have to advertise. I move in Monday." My Motorola NSU parking was free.

I came home to my dad and said, "Dad, I straightened out my book with the radio. And on top of it, guess what?

I'm moving out Monday." He said, "How the heck did you do that?" Then I told him the story, that this happened, that I was just lucky. On Monday, I moved in there. I was twenty-one years old and had only a motor scooter, but my friend (Horst Koblitz) had an old '36 Fiat convertible, so we put my three suitcases in there, and he helped me move.

When I arrived, I said to the lady, "Who else lives here?" "Well," she said, "my husband and I, we are in the electrical business. He's an electrician. He works on construction, and he lives in the room in the basement because he likes to read a lot. We have only one daughter, and she lives with me upstairs. Down here is your room, and then we have one married couple. And then there is one room occupied by two single girls." That was interesting! I said to my friend, "I don't know who these girls are, but we need to look and investigate." So then I moved in. My friend, Horst Koblitz, was a friend from Hamburg. We went out together once in a while, and we all looked for girls, you know. We'd go dancing and have fun.

One Sunday morning, I heard the girls out in the kitchen. One of the girls' names was Sieglinde (Linda). Linda and her cousin Helga had a gas stove in their room. They would make coffee there. They also had their own breakfast. The girls didn't eat in the landlord's kitchen. They wanted the cheapest rent like me, so they didn't pay extra to eat. Mrs. Milow, the landlord, had breakfast with their daughter.

Anyway, on Sunday morning Linda came out and said, "Mrs. Milow, I'd like to show you my new dress," and she turned around. I overheard that in my room. This was all in the kitchen, and it was early in the morning, so I figured it was time now to meet these girls.

I put my jacket on and acted like I had to go and take my motorcycle out. I looked at her, and she looked at me, and it was just like that (Peter snapping fingers). I said, "Oh, that dress is nice. I love it. You look good in the dress." Then we talked a little bit. She said, "How long have you been here?" And I said, "Only two weeks." Then I asked her, "What do you do?" She said her first job was with the Hamburg city police as a secretary. She had to do shorthand and all that kind of stuff, but only in German, not in English.

Then she introduced me to her cousin, Helga. She was a seamstress. They both worked in Hamburg. After a short time went by, I asked Linda to go out to a movie with me, and she loved that. We went out, we walked around, and we became very close. We loved each other. After a while, Helga decided she would like to move out. She figured Linda and me were getting very close together. So she had her room, and I had my room there, and that's the way it was, nice.

Usually, according to German law at this time, you have until ten o'clock that you can visit the girls' room, or the girls can visit you. By ten o'clock, it's quiet time, and you have to be back in your apartment, so we did that. We went by the rules.

But one day, I sneaked over to her room at night, and we were together there. There was somebody who wanted to break into the garage where the electrician had his tools in the shop. It was behind the house. The landlord's daughter was upstairs when the alarm went off. The garage was all wired up for security.

The alarm went off, and she didn't know there was a break-in. She called, "Fire, fire, fire!" She heard the alarm going and figured there was a fire in the house, because they had fire alarms in the house, as well, but it really came from the break-in.

However, there I was in Linda's room. And, of course, the mother and the daughter came down in the kitchen. I had no other choice but to jump out of Linda's window. We were on the first floor, so it was not so high. I jumped out and told Linda to jump, too, because, "There's a fire." And so, Linda jumped, too. Not into my arms, she missed it, but it was no problem.

When we were out, the crooks must have seen us. I didn't know there were crooks there, but they took off. Mr. Milow came from downstairs and said, "My God, it's good that you came out so quick." He patted me on the shoulder and said, "Good guy, good work." So that was one episode.

But Mr. Milow himself, he was a very educated person. He was a master electrician. He was once sick with a nervous breakdown, and they brought him to the hospital. When he came into the emergency room, the doctor said to Mrs. Milow, "What is your husband doing? Is he some kind of a professor? What is his profession?" She said, "No, he's a master electrician, but he reads and studies a lot in the library downstairs. He doesn't watch much television." The doctor said, "He's really overeducated." That's the only time we heard it from her. He was okay. After a while, he was healthy again.

One day, he called me into his library, and we talked about America, and I showed him my papers that I filled out for my visa. He said, "Don't you have a good job here? You have a good future here as well." I agreed, but it would be nice to see something else.

So then in the meantime, my friend Horst Koblitz and I were looking to work for Lufthansa German Airlines. We both applied and went through screening and aptitude tests in 1955-56. Both of us passed, but while great opportunities were presented to us, they also wanted us to sign an employment contract. Schooling for the job would be free of charge; the company would "invest in you." In return, you would have to agree to work for them for three years after the schooling. If you agreed to this and later changed your mind, you would be responsible for paying back all of the costs for schooling and their investment in you.

I asked my dad what he thought about this arrangement, and he replied something like, "It's up to you. You are old enough to decide; it's your future." I did not sign the employment contract. However, my friend Horst did, and I'm sure he did very well with them. I didn't ever regret this decision, as I was sure I wanted to come to the U.S. and knew that I'd be happy and do well in my new venture.

Anyway, the radio company I worked for was bought out by another company in Cologne, and they decided to do different marketing. They didn't want any more direct distributors, so then I had a different job.

When I told my then-girlfriend, Sieglinde, that I got my visa to travel to the U.S., she told me that she thought she was pregnant, but she quickly added that since I had my visa, I should go. I promised her that if I didn't like it there, I would return right away. If I did like it there, I would send for her to come over, too. That's the way we decided. So I was in the States about a month when Linda wrote me a letter that she went to a doctor and found out she was pregnant, and that was it.

Now, her mother and all her relatives were very upset. They said, "That guy has probably skipped the country." And good thing that happened while I was in the U.S. already, because if her mother would have known that I planned to leave, you never know how the Germans and U.S. Consulate would have reacted.

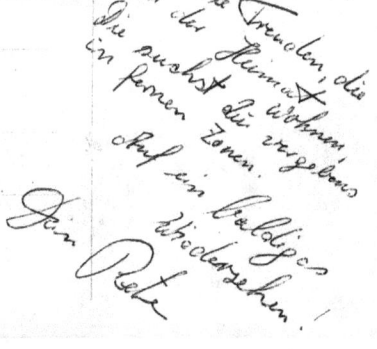

LETTER FROM PETER
TO SIEGLINDE
English Translation:
*The happiness that lives in the
Homeland, is also sought out
in far-away places...
Here's to a reunion soon!
Your Peter*

Linda could have decided against my leaving. It was up to her. If the officials knew that I was leaving under these circumstances, they might not have let me out of the country. The Consulate would say, "No, you cannot leave the country. You have a girl that's pregnant," and that would be a strike against me! But Linda loved me and let it be. She knew that I would come back, or she would come over the large pond. We made a promise to each other to stay together.

It was February 12, 1957 that I arrived in New York, and two days later by train I arrived in Milwaukee. My mother and brothers arrived two weeks ahead of me. There was a large family reunion party with all of the relatives. My Uncle Carl sponsored for all six of us: my three brothers, my mother,

Arrival from Germany to the US and greeted by Carl and his family. Pictured from left to right—Uncle Carl's daughter, Beverly Schulz, Klaus and Guenter, and aunt Anna Klawonn.

Reunion captured by the Milwaukee *Journal Sentinal*, 2-12-1957.

her sister (Anna), and myself. My Uncle Carl and the sisters were together after thirty-five years. I met my mother's cousin, Kathryn Lemke (Schulz). Her father arrived in New Jersey in the early 1900s and was successful with his sawmill. Kathryn and her husband, Arthur, had no children, only a doggie named Lucky. They were so happy to see us all, and so were we. But since I was already in the U.S., nobody knew about Linda and the pregnancy. After a few weeks went by, I talked to my Uncle Carl first, not to my mother. I wanted to talk to a man.

Pictured from left to right—Uncle Carl's son,
Eric Schulz, and aunt Anna Klawonn.

This is a happy homecoming photo of Meta Jentzsch with her brother Carl Schulz, who had already come to the US years prior. In the forefront, Carl's daughter, Beverly.

My uncle understood and could speak German perfect. I talked to him about the situation with Linda, and he said he was in the same boat with his wife, Irma. Irma was already pregnant when they were married, but they wanted to get married anyway. He said, "If you love her, marry her," but he also said he could not sponsor any more people, because his finances were limited. The law is this way. But he said, "Your mother's cousin, Kathryn Lemke Schulz, and Arthur are in Milwaukee. Their parents came from Germany, too. They have no children. We can talk to them. Financially, they have no problem. They go every year to Vegas and have fun. I'm sure they would like to sponsor for Sieglinde (Linda)."

My mother's cousin, Kathryn, was the daughter of Uncle Reinhold, who had the sawmill in New Jersey. He let Frieda, who was pregnant at the time, live by him. They had no children at this time. So Uncle Carl said, "Let me talk to Arthur and Kathryn to see if they'd like to sponsor Linda." They talked, and then Uncle Carl took me there. They said, "We would love to sponsor her. We have no kids, only a doggie. And if she's pregnant," he said, "you better let the child be born in Germany, because they have better insurance there. If we sponsor her now and she's pregnant and the child is born here, and some complications happen, then it could be very expensive for us."

In Germany, you don't have that. If the child is born in Germany, Linda would be covered by the insurance, and she could work so many weeks before she has the baby. Then she would have sick benefits and all that. Arthur said he would sponsor both of them. He loved that. It was better that way. I said, "Yes, you're right," because the insurance is not like they have over there, but that's the way we do it. I was so happy and thanked Kathryn and Arthur many times over. So then I wrote Linda a letter and told her somebody else would sponsor her from our family.

Linda was only eighteen years old as I reached out and asked her to leave her homeland and come to me in the U.S. She obliged. We were truly in love. Arthur and Kathryn immediately started the sponsorship process for Linda and the baby Ulrich, nickname "Uli." Love is stronger than any borders, and we did spend time apart, during which my first son was born.

Linda was healthy and educated to work in the future. I had saved money for the airline ticket for Linda and son Uli to come over to the U.S. Uli was born on September 30, 1957, and Linda arrived with Ulrich Michael in December 1957. The sponsorship went pretty quick and without any problems. It was a beautiful day in Chicago. There was sunshine, and in Wisconsin there was snow. A friend of mine picked us up in the car. I didn't have a car then, not even a motor scooter. Linda and I were married in January 1958 at Mader's Restaurant in Milwaukee.

We all came to Milwaukee and lived in my mother's apartment on Mitchell Street. We all shared the apartment: my three brothers, my mother and her sister, and my family. It had four bedrooms and one shower. I moved in with them for maybe two or four weeks, and we made it. I had one room, and my mother cooked. Linda only took care of Uli. There were three women and one stove, but Linda was smart enough. She let my Aunt Anna and my mother do what they wanted to, and she just took care of Uli, and everything was very good.

There were also in-laws from Ruth Gleisner's that had an apartment in Milwaukee that was furnished completely. It had beds and everything. They moved back to Arizona when they retired, Ruth Zeidelhack's (now Gleisner) in-laws, and they said, "The apartment is now available. We're moving out."

We went over there and talked to the landlord. It would be the ideal thing because we had no furniture and no credit established. It would be good to move there, so we went over there to see the apartment. It was on National Avenue. We introduced ourselves and met these people. The landlord said that they were already informed by the Gliesners that they were going to move out. My uncle told the landlord, "If you don't mind, we have relatives here: a wife, husband, and one little boy. They'd like to move in there." "Oh," she said, "wonderful. As long as they are clean people."

The apartment had a fridge and a little kitchen with a stove. The washing machine was on a different floor for the whole apartment. There were a lot of people living there, maybe five or six couples, but there were no kids in there. We were the only one with a child. So we lived there. We saved our money. We paid $25 a week. Sometimes we only made $57 to $60 a week take-home pay net, but Linda knew how to save money.

We paid the rent every week on time. I also had part-time jobs, and everything worked out. We saved some money. Then

I bought an NSU motor scooter. That was the only thing that I could afford. When we went shopping, somebody would watch Uli, and when we went to the store, we'd put everything in the motor scooter. But that was not good. My brother said, "You need to buy a car." I bought an Isetta, a used BMW, just a little thing. Three people could sit in it. The doors opened in the front. Anyway, at least we had a little more room, so we could all three sit in there. But then after a while, I bought a different car. The Isetta would break down all the time, and the mechanic told me to get rid of it. It was a used vehicle.

So I decided to buy a new car Volkswagen from Concourse Motors. They were on Oakland Avenue in Milwaukee. We wanted to buy a Ford. We looked at a dealership on North Avenue. I was excited, and I dreamed about taking one. It had two exhausts through the bumper and lots of room. Cool! I dreamt to take the car, and then my family and I would travel to Hamburg and drive the big car on vacation. They called it "Show-Off" in American cars. But then we found out the price was $3,500. I came down to Earth.

We went and checked our budget, but we couldn't afford it. Linda was a good manager with our finances, but there wasn't enough money, and we needed a car. So I said, "What is the next thing?" I don't want old, used stuff anymore, because it was too much of a problem. Other friends had problems with used cars, and I had problems with mine. No way. I had bought a Volkswagen. It was $1,900 new with a sunroof. We could afford that in the budget. But the only thing was, you had to wait six months for it. And so we waited. We used the bus.

Finally, the new car came, and then we drove it on vacation. The first vacation we took was to the Wisconsin Dells. My mother watched the children. We had Angelika at that time, so we had two children then. By then, the apartment was actually too small. When Angie was little, we had the crib, and it was okay.

But then the landlady talked to us and said now that we had two children, the apartment building was only for adults – couples or older people. "I like you," she said and, "I don't want to throw you out, but just look for something for the future. You can take a month or two, three months, makes no difference." Mrs. Patthauer, the landlady, was a nice person and understanding. And we understood that. We said, "Okay, we will find something."

Then we found an apartment that we rented. We had enough savings, so we bought some new furniture. We bought the furniture in Chicago, and I still have that furniture today. We bought a washing machine, dryer, stove, and refrigerator, all from Sears. Sears was the first with credit cards, so we built our credit up.

At this time, I worked for American Motors. When we came over here, Linda had to learn English. Her jobs in Germany and here were completely different. She had to learn shorthand in English and the keypunch operation. They didn't have that in Germany at that time, but the keypunch went worldwide after a while. That was before they came out with computers. But typewriters for her were no problem. She knew how to type, organize, etc.

Linda went to the school for two years, and afterwards, her first job was at the Woolworth accounting office. She really liked her first job. During the day, I watched the kids, and at night I worked at American Motors in Milwaukee. Before Linda came over, I went to school to learn English already while she was still in Germany.

One day at American Motors, I was laid off. The company was not stable, so there were a lot of times I was laid off. There were always wildcat strikes with the union. So one day we had in mind to buy a duplex. We figured if we lived upstairs or downstairs, then we could rent it out. I wanted to get it financed, but we couldn't because the banks told me that, "The company where you work is not stable, and your wife just got a job." So we forgot about it. We decided not to buy a duplex and kept on renting.

Linda had a job, and I was laid off. I worked part-time for the owners of Schlitz Brewing Co. I asked if I could work there part-time, and they said, "What can you do?" "Well, I can do everything – grass-cutting, etc." Ms. Uihlein had a huge house, and there was a lot of stuff to do outside. Then she said, "Can you wash cars, wax cars? I'm very particular with my car." I said, "Yes, I like cars." So I got a job there.

Another buddy that I had in Milwaukee, he worked at American Motors, and we both started there. And, of course, they always pay with a check, and that helped us make our payments, because we were laid off and received only an unemployment payment from American Motors.

We started in the morning at nine o'clock and worked until

five o'clock. So then, when you get paid part-time with a check and you collect unemployment, that was against the law. When I went to the unemployment office, they called me one day, and they said, "You got to come in." They said to me, "Do you collect unemployment from American Motors?" I said, "Yes." And they said, "You work part-time, and you cannot do that, because that's against the law. Somebody called in here, one of your countrymen because I know he had the same accent, and we have to report you." So I said, "That's nice to know." But he said, "I know how it is. It's tough times, and you have a family, and you have to pay your bills, but I have no other choice. I have to report this case!"

We had the car, and on the first day Linda started her job, Monday morning, I was supposed to drive her to work. Linda was so happy that she had a job after all of the schooling that she had. The new landlady upstairs was German, too. We watched their kids when the landlady worked. The husband worked, too. And when I drove Linda to work, they'd watch our kids. The kids were all the same age.

One day, there was a knock on the door, and there were two policemen. They said to me, "We have to arrest you." I said, "For what?" And he said, "Well, so and so from the unemployment office said you made illegal income." "Oh, my God," I said. He said I had to go to the courthouse.

And I said, "My wife just started a job, and if she doesn't show up today, I don't think that she would have that job anymore." Then both officers came in the house, and they saw that everything was nice and clean, and they saw our kids, Angie and Uli. Then he said, "Well, I tell you what, if you are there at nine o'clock, we will let you go and won't take you in. You can drive your wife to work. You are reasonable people. But," he said, "you have to be at the courthouse in Milwaukee by nine o'clock." I said, "Okay, I will be there."

Anyhow, I drove Linda to her job, and I said to her, "I don't know what they will do, if we will get a fine or something. But it makes no difference. The landlady said she would watch the kids while I'm gone." Linda had to be to work by eight o'clock, and I made it by nine o'clock to the courthouse. They put me in jail with all the drunks they picked up off the street. I talked to the fella, and I said, "This is impossible. I didn't do anything like all of these people here." He said, "Keep your mouth shut. You'll get your turn when you come out." So I didn't say nothing anymore. It did not pay off.

Eventually, they called me to go in the courtroom, and then he asked if there was anybody in here who knows me. There was one guy; he was a tavern owner on Lisbon Avenue. We went there once in a while and had sausage and beer. I knew him pretty well. Anyway, he was on jury duty, and he had to go out.

Then the Judge said, "Guilty or not guilty?" I said, "Well, if it's against the law, then I'm guilty, because I didn't know. I wanted to make money, so then I'm guilty." The judge said, "So why did you do it?" I said, "We came over here. We tried to make ends meet. We have bills to pay – our refrigerator, furniture to pay for, and I have an automobile which I have to pay for. With the part-time job and with my unemployment, I could just get by. I could pay everything."

"Well," he said, "okay." He put the hammer down. "You get a $200 fine, and you can pay it off." The judge stopped my unemployment, so I didn't get anything anymore, and I agreed and was free to go. But Linda had a job at least. She had a job, but I got no unemployment money, so I was in a squeeze.

Now, I never forgot the General Motors Acceptance Corporation. That's where we had the automobile financed at that time. That was my second car. We traded in the Volkswagen for an Opel from GMC. It was bigger and had a bigger trunk. So I called them up and said, "I cannot pay the payments at the moment for that car. You have to work with me somehow before American Motors hires us back again. If the model change is over, I'll go back to work, and then I can pay you. My wife just got a new job. Income is coming in, but at the moment, my unemployment has stopped. I got a fine because I worked part-time." I told them the story. So he said, "Well, then we have to pick up your car." I said, "If you have to pick up the car, that's fine. I will take the bus. Come and get the key."

It was twenty or thirty minutes later when they called back, and he said, "We don't want that car. We won't come and pick it up. We'll work with you because you always paid good. We understand your situation, and if you pay a little bit, we will wait two months and then we see what happens." So I got to keep my car.

After that, I went back to American Motors. The work was good, but I wanted to get out of American Motors in the worst way. I said to Linda, "You have a job at Woolworth accounting office. I will go back in sales, because I don't want to do factory work at American Motors anymore, especially when they are not stable. There is no future there."

Time went by, and one day a salesman from Kirby vacuum cleaners came to our house and wanted to show us his vacuum unit. We agreed and made an appointment. We needed a vacuum cleaner. The salesman came with a Kirby vacuum cleaner, and he showed me the machine after the demo. I said, "What is the deal on that Kirby?" And he said, "Well, so and so."

I said, "If there is financing, I don't want financing. I want three months like cash." He said, "Okay." I got a decent deal out of him, so I bought it. I looked the machine over, and I said to Linda, "It's a wonderfully constructed machine. It's well engineered. It's a wonderful unit. I wouldn't mind selling that myself. It really sells itself, it's so well-made."

So I called the company on Hopkins Street and spoke to Fritz Schneider. He was a distributor for Kirby. There were only two distributors, him and one other. Fritz Schneider had the territory of Milwaukee and the vicinity out there. I called him up and said, "I bought a Kirby. I received financing at your office, and I will keep it for ninety days like cash." I said, "I like the quality of the machine. It's really good. Do you need any salesmen?" "Oh," he said, "my God, we always need good salesmen. Did you ever sell something?" I said, "Yes, I sold in Germany. Of course, here I didn't. I worked for American Motors and did side jobs, but I'd like to go into sales. I won't stay at American Motors."

He said, "Come down here and see us on Sunday. You are invited to come to my home. Bring the whole family." He wanted to meet Linda and the kids, so I came with the family. They made chicken dinner, and we talked for hours. He said, "You can start tomorrow if you want to." I said, "I've got the kids, and I have to have insurance like at American Motors. What kind of insurance do you have?" Well, he said they cannot match that. He said he can get insurance, but it's different insurance than what American Motors has, of course. American Motors is a huge company.

At that time, insurance was free at American Motors. In Europe, we paid 50% for our health insurance, and the employer paid 50%. That is federal law, but everyone had insurance. At American Motors, we paid for our health insurance. It was deducted from our paycheck. But the union worked it out later so that you didn't have to pay anymore for health insurance, which didn't benefit the company, but that's the way it was. The health insurance was free.

Then I worked for Schneider. I asked, "Can I start working for you in a week?" and I gave notice at American Motors. I told American Motors, "I need two weeks unpaid leave of absence." They said, "All right, we can give you that." Within those two weeks, I made good money. I sold machines. Fritz trained me. I went with a couple guys to sell Kirbys. Then I started to get appointments myself. They had appointments from the restaurant show and the State Fair and other areas. I went there and demonstrated and sold the machine. I did well and earned my commission. Everything was on commission. It was wonderful.

So then I went back to American Motors. I had to go back,

because the insurance was still in effect there. I worked another month during the day (second shift) for AMC, but then I worked part-time in the evening for Schneider, since most of the time you have to show the machine in the evening. For health insurance reasons, I asked AMC for three more weeks of leave of absence.

And then the fella said to me, "What do you want to do?" That was in the office of American Motors. He was a decent guy, too. I said, "I tell you what. I want to leave American Motors because of these strikes here. Employees have to go along with the union, and you have no other choice." I said, "There is no opportunity. You cannot even get a house financed working here."

He said to me, "I hear you. This isn't the place for you. You better quit." I said, "You're right." They gave me one more week. But then somebody else higher up called me into the office and said that with all the time on and off, he said, "We can't do that, you have to quit today." So I said, "I quit right now." I asked them to send me my check next week, and I went full-time at Schneider Kirby of Milwaukee – Division of Scott & Fetzer – Ohio.

I was working for Schneider full-time. He guaranteed $200 a week, plus commission. But the next week, if you have a lot of sales, they'd deduct it. Schneider called it "a draw against commission." I said I didn't want to do that anymore because if I know I can sell, I didn't want a draw. "I will only work on commission." "That's fine."

I worked for Fritz Schneider for a while, and then he promoted me. He asked if I would like to go to his office in Racine. He opened a new office on Goold Street. "You can manage that office for me, sales and service in Racine and Racine County. Racine County is your territory." I agreed and said, "Okay." He said, "Your wife can take over the office part-time while she's working for Woolworth. You can take care of the sales. Linda is good with bookwork, so she can help you. My wife does that, too. Your wife can do it alone at the start. We'll pay you for management, plus 10% commission on the repairs, parts, or whatever you sell, plus your commission on the Kirby sales."

I agreed and said, "That's a good deal." He said, "If you move down there, I will pay the moving costs. You just need to find an apartment." So we looked for an apartment, but we couldn't find the right thing right away. Then we found a house and put $1,000 down. I said to Linda, "You know what? Let's buy a house instead of an apartment. Having a bank mortgage would be okay. It will be our own house then."

Even though I wasn't with Kirby very long, I worked so many years at American Motors, and they wouldn't approve a mortgage. But with my new job, they agreed to finance the house. We could buy it. The house sale was from a divorce case. It was located near Goold Street in the area around Rapids Drive (where Zayres was). It was behind Zayres. Also, Park High School was in that area. Since the sale involved a divorce case, the deal dragged along.

In November, Schneider said to me, "Look, by the first of December you've got to move the furniture out. You only have until the thirtieth to live in Milwaukee, and then you've got to be out." He had to order a moving truck before the end of the month to move to Racine. I was under a lot of stress to find a place to move to. I said, "Fritz, we're looking for a place. Sooner or later, we will find something."

Two days before I went out to the house in Racine, the seller hadn't moved out yet. They waited until midnight the next day, so they were out legally. She wanted to sell the home and was still living in it. "I had to order the moving company in Milwaukee, and you've got to get moving in two days. You're not moved out, and you have a thousand excuses, the divorce case and so on." I told her the deal was off.

Then they said, "You don't get your down payment back." I said, "We'll wait and see." I said, "I will go and get myself a lawyer." Somebody told me about a good lawyer in Racine, and I told her the whole story. She said, "That's all right. I'll get some money back for you. She got the down payment back. Of course, I had to pay her, too, but I didn't lose everything.

So I looked in the paper. I saw a house for rent in Sturtevant. When I went down there to see it, the builder, Herbert Katt, said to me, "It's a model home. I've got my office on the top level. Everything else is there. The washing machine is already there. We use it ourselves. There is a kitchen and stove, but we don't cook. Everything is like new."

I said, "Well, how much do you want for it?" He said about 150, but it was very high to rent the whole house. And I said, "My God, for that money I can buy a house." "Well," he said, "would you like to buy it? It has been for sale for a long time, and I couldn't sell it." It was the biggest house in Sturtevant. But he said, "If you would like to buy it, I will sell it to you now." So I said, "How much is it?"

He said, "You can take a mortgage for fifteen, twenty, or thirty years, and we will figure it all out." I said, "That's a good deal. I think my wife will like that house. It's beautiful. It's a new style, much better than the other place. Here is a hundred bucks. I'll take it." I told him about the other home in Racine that I walked away from. Then we started working on the legal papers the next day.

I said, "I will bring my wife tomorrow so she can see it." And he said, "Okay. That's fine. I'll be here." Then he said, "But you've got to paint it inside complete (it was a model home) because we have a lot of pictures on the walls. You will need to paint the upstairs and downstairs. But if you paint it yourself, I'll give you a credit for it." I said, "Yes, I will do that all myself. Give me a credit of $2,000 to paint the whole house inside." He said, "That is extra down payment for you." I said, "Yeah, that sounds good." So the deal went through. Linda looked at the house in Sturtevant the next day, and she said, "Oh, I love it." But about the Racine house, she said, "I didn't like the other house. It was not clean enough, and I would have to do so much cleaning."

Then I told Fritz Schneider, "Move us to Sturtevant." The house was empty, and we just moved our furniture in. And that's the way we came to Racine, in Sturtevant. The house is still there. It's still nice. I don't know what the price on the house is yet. The house was reasonable, but it was a lot of money at that time. People would ask us, "How can you afford that?" I said, "Look, in Milwaukee the houses are much more expensive. Down here they are cheaper, and so we bought it. That's why."

At that time, the house was the biggest one on the whole

block. It was very nice. Downstairs was the kitchen and living room, and upstairs there were three bedrooms and the family room. There was one bathroom upstairs. After a while, we made an office in the garage and a 1/2 bathroom downstairs.

The address of the house was 3149 Buckingham Road, Sturtevant. Once Linda's mother came from Germany to visit us, and she stayed in that house. Her mother came to the States two times. Her sisters and brothers came, also, for my daughters' weddings.

Linda was very happy to have her own home. She was always behind me, so she quit at the Woolworth accounting office and helped me in the business.

One day, Fritz Schneider told me he was actually disappointed that I bought a house. And I said, "Why, Fritz?" At that time, we had Olaf. Olaf was born in Racine. Fritz and his wife, Clara, were the godparents. They both came from Germany, too. But I said to Fritz, "Okay. How come you are disappointed? I mean, it's so nice having a house, because," I said, "the rent was higher than the house payment, and I don't like to pay rent if I can buy a house."

He said, "I understand that, but I have other plans for you." I said to him, "What do you mean? Why didn't you tell me that before?" He said, "I want you to go to Mequon, Wisconsin and get a house. It's bigger territory, and there is a larger store. You could have that one there instead of here in Racine, or you can keep both of them, because I would like to retire."

His wife, Clara, had arthritis in her arms, and they went to Arizona for a month. The doctor in Milwaukee told her go to

Arizona and retire, and Fritz said, "Well, it's time to retire." So they went to Arizona, but she had more pain in her arms than in Milwaukee. The doctor there said, "Who the heck sent you down here?" And they said, "Well, the doctor in Milwaukee told me I've got to go to a dryer climate." He said, "You have a different arthritis. There are two types. One is for dry, and the one you have needs warm, moist air. You need Florida." They came back from Arizona, and they went to Florida instead.

They liked Florida. The pain was less and much better for her. So then they said, "Okay, we'll sell the Racine office to you," but the Mequon office he sold to someone else, because I was stuck in Racine with the house. I had Racine and Racine County. I could not sell in Milwaukee at all. Any leads that we had, they were all for these people in Milwaukee.

Racine was okay. We won some sales contests and certain things, but of course not all of them. It's a blue-collar area in Racine, and it was a little different, but we still made a pretty good living. I had a lot of commercial accounts there, like hospitals, and I also had the Playboy Club in Lake Geneva and other resorts, too. All the resorts, I sold them vacuum cleaners, and I made my rounds with them. We had two salesmen and a sales manager.

After a while, Uli was old enough, so he and his friend Rick from Case High School, they both were able to help. Uli cleaned the store and helped decorating the windows. They made extra money just like any teenager does while on vacation, and they liked that. They would sell used vacuum cleaners at the 7 Mile Fair.

At the hospitals, we sold the Kirby machines, but they said, "We have intensive care customers, and these Kirbys make too much noise. We cannot have that. We need wet/dry vacuum cleaners in operation rooms. If you have that, we would love to buy them from you because of your good service." But Kirby didn't make any for these facilities.

So I hunted around. I called the Chicago distributor for Hild Commercial Vacuum Cleaner Co. and they said, "We have nobody in Racine County. We would love to have you as a distributor." I agreed and said, "Good, we can do that. I will buy your machines and have the Racine area." So I bought their wet/dry machines. I also bought a very quiet one from Denmark that had double filters for hospital use. So I had these two extra machines and the Kirby in my store.

Then, when the supervisor came from Kirby one day, he saw these machines in there, and he said, "What kind of machines are these? You have trade-ins?" I said, "No, they're not trade-ins, they're brand-new ones. I sell them to the hospitals." "Well, you cannot have that here. It's Kirby only."

I said, "That's correct, but Kirby does not make this type of machine, and I've got to satisfy my customer. If I don't have them, they will buy them someplace else. I can make just as much or more with these big machines than with the Kirby, and it helps to pay the overhead." "Well," he said, "I cannot allow that. You have to take them out." We got in an argument, and I said to him, "Ask the Kirby company who pays the rent here and who pays for local advertising."

We continued arguing, and he said, "Then you're done

with Kirby." I said, "Fine." So we quit with Kirby. He said, "You have thirty days to take off the Kirby signs for sales and service and take it out of the paper and off the cars. You've got to find yourself a new company name." That's how we started Racine Vacuum Center. That was the new name. I took "Kirby" off. I could sell all of the Kirbys I had, but I couldn't get new Kirbys anymore. We did all of the same service, etc.

At the same time, there was a big distributor in Florida. Schaefer was a Lutheran minister by trade, however, he also was a Kirby distributor. He was the biggest distributor in the whole state of Florida. He and some of his friends developed a machine that looked like the Kirby, only it was more advanced.

He contacted Scott and Fetzer, the company that owns Kirby. It's a big corporation. They traded on the Wall Street stock market, and Kirby is one of their divisions. They owned paint and knife companies as well. He contacted them and wanted to sell them the machine. He said, "Look, I invented it. I want my patent. You can buy me out. I want so much for the machine. It's a better machine than the Kirby is," and so on. Scott and Fetzer said, "No, we don't want that." So he said, "Well, if you don't want it, I will build it myself and will build a factory."

So he quit Kirby, and he was one of the biggest distributors the company had. They had distributors all over the nation, and in Canada. But the one in Florida was actually the biggest one. Then we found out that he quit Kirby. He sent one guy to Sturtevant with a big RV, and he said, "I want to talk to you. I want you as a distributor for us." He called it the Bison company. That was their trademark.

We agreed and asked, "What kind of guarantee do you have? What is the machine all about?" He had a machine along, and he showed me the Bison. Everything was more modern. I said, "That's a wonderful machine," but nobody knew about it. It's brand new. He said, "Yeah, but we also have engineers from Germany on our team. We have Pfaff sewing machines as partners. We plan to build a factory in Ocala, Florida. That's where we will make the Bison. But the gears in the front of the vacuum, they're all driven from Switzerland."

The machine was okay. We went with them, signed their contract, and they said, "You can come down to Florida for training." So me and Linda went down to Florida for the first time. We had never gone there before. It was nice to see palms and all of that in the southern state.

When we were in Florida, I told them not to tell us how to sell Bisons. We knew how to sell Kirbys, so we could sell Bisons. We just wanted them to tell us the mechanical side of it, how to repair it, and what was involved with it. The guarantee was one year. We ended up with a large territory, half the state of Wisconsin, including Milwaukee County.

At that time, I invested $2,000 in stock at Bison. When we started with them, we were so happy with the machine. Linda said maybe we should invest more than $2,000, then we'd have more in the company. I said, "Wait a while. $2,000 is enough."

Suddenly, they got in an argument with the Pfaff fella from Germany. Pfaff is a big company. They make big sewing machines. They made the gear boxes for the Bison vacuum. After this, Schaefer started making these gear boxes in Florida, but the gear boxes were cheap. We found that out when we sold the machines here. There was a one-year guarantee from the factory, and we added an extra year from us when we sold it in our territory so our customers would have a two-year guarantee. Compared to Kirby, you only had one year.

Each gear box costs $25 to $30 wholesale. But then the gear boxes didn't hold up, so we sent them back to the company. I said, "They don't last long, only six months," and we asked them to send us new replacements. We asked, "Why don't you have these gear boxes like they used to be?" We never got a good answer from them. Anyway, the gear boxes didn't hold up. We had to replace them after a while. Then we got a letter saying that they're not replacing gear boxes anymore. "You're on your own."

Then the machines were not like they used to be. And Linda was, of course, in the office all of the time, so she knew. Then all of a sudden, they said to me, "Peter, we have to have a meeting. We are operating in the red instead of black. That costs us too much money. We replace all these things free of charge. We cannot sell them anymore." I agreed and said, "No, we can't."

I called Schaefer up at that time, and I told him "I'll take my $2,000 out," but I couldn't get it out. So I went by Riegelman, my attorney (we still have him today), and I said, "Bob, take a look at our stock, the $2,000." He said, "You know what? There's nothing you can do. You can take it to the toilet."

The German company, Pfaff, ended the partnership and got their stocks and money out from Bison. After Pfaff left, Bison went bankrupt, and the stockholders and distributors were in the red. So we decided not to buy Bisons anymore. Those we had, we fixed up, sold, or traded for other machines just to keep our customers happy. After Bison went down, I said to Linda, "Now, we will only sell other machines." We had other machines like Danish machines for hospitals, and we forgot about Bison because that company brought us down in the red.

We had that another six months or a year, and then we decided to sell the vacuum business. I had all of the financial records, what we sold to all of these commercial accounts, and we had good accounts. The business was okay. The orders came for machines already for January, February, and March the following year, but I could not deliver them because their budget for that year was filled by the hospitals. They said the PO's delivered in the next year in January.

We didn't own the store, we rented it, but I wanted to sell the business that year. Then we had a customer who said to me that he wanted to buy the company. His wife worked in the phone company. I don't know his name anymore, but anyway, he wanted to buy the company, and it was okay. He had one child that he adopted. He needed to have a business or something steady with good income in order to adopt the child, and that likely was the reason that he wanted to buy the business.

I told him, "Come in, and I will train you. I will introduce you to all of the commercial customers I have." He said, "I don't need that." He knew it all. He said, "I take it over in January." So I gave him all of the PO contracts for the machines that had to be delivered. Everything went with the sale. "All of the money is yours because you buy the whole company with the machines, but you get it back right away in January when you deliver them. You get instant income, plus you repair and service the account."

Now, I asked, "Do you want to finance?" Well, he didn't have a finance company. Our bank, the Bank of Elmwood, they knew the business, what money came in, and so they took the chance on financing him. Our business was okay yet. It showed a profit. We only went in the red with the Bison a year ago.

So he bought the whole thing, and Elmwood Bank financed it. But after a while, he was top-heavy. In a year, the hospital in Kenosha called me once (that was Mr. Schmidt), and he asked me, "You know, Peter, I hate to bother you. I know you sold the business, but I had your phone number here. Do you know where that guy is?" I said, "What do you mean? Doesn't he have the store open?" "Well," he said, "he picked the machines up from us to service them, but he never brought them back."

I went down to the store, and there was a big sign that said "On vacation, up in Canada fishing." I called Schmidt back and said, "Schmidt, it's terrible. I never knew this would happen." He said, "That never happened with you because you were always there, but now we cannot do anything." He said, "Don't worry about it. I'm glad that you checked it out. We didn't like that guy anyhow."

Then he bought new machines from the competition someplace else. When that guy came back, Schmidt called me back and said he brought all his machines back after two weeks.

Schmidt told him, "You know, we have to clean the hospital." "I was on vacation." He said, "Yes, you go on vacation, but not on our time. What do you think we clean the hospital with? We bought other machines. All these machines that you had repaired, you can sell them for whatever you got for it. We are done." He threw him out of his office. So it didn't take long, and he went bankrupt. I talked to Charles Meyer at that time at the Bank of Elmwood, and Charles said we didn't get the money. However, in two years, we received the loan money.

After we sold the vacuum cleaner business, we went on to sell Swiffy, a spot remover. We went all over the country to sell it at home shows, state fairs, and so on. Then we heard that they developed a metal polish that is a polish for every metal in Germany. You can use it on silver and steel. When I heard about that, I figured I had to go investigate. We found the German chemist in Germany. I went over to Germany three times with Linda. We got samples, and it worked very good. We tested it here in Wisconsin.

Then they told us, "Well, don't put your hopes too high." Not that they didn't want us to sell it, but in the States maybe it's hard to sell because they have one polish for every metal. They have a silver polish, brass polish, stainless steel polish, and so on. For each metal, they have one polish just like we had here years ago, but now they have one for everything. I figured it would sell because it's cheaper to buy one polish for everything. But of course, we said we will try it once. We brought it over here and tried to sell the product. We still had the Swiffy at that time before we had the Flitz.

When we came back, we tested it here, and everybody we gave it to, they loved it. Flitz was only developed for interior use, so we figured we had to make it so that it works for interior and exterior use. There was not enough protective coating in it for exterior use, so we figured, well, we have to go back to the drawing board in Germany.

We had a good meeting over there with the chemist and a friend of mine, Willie. The result: yes, we can do that, but it costs about $30,000 to do it all over again for the interior and commercial exterior. I said, "The funds of $30,000 we don't have. I've got to go to the bank and borrow that money somehow."

When we flew back to the States, we had a meeting with the banks. We tried several banks in Racine, and nobody wanted to give us a loan on polish. They said, "Well, if something goes wrong, we cannot sell polish. We are in the banking business." I realized that, but that's the way it was. They all turned us down because we have no track record of that. I only told them how good it is, but that was not enough for the banks at that time.

However, there was one bank, the Bank of Elmwood in Racine. We dealt with them years before with the vacuum cleaner business and also with Swiffy spot remover. They agreed that we can do the loan. "If you are sold on it so much, then of course we should give you a loan. However, we have to use your house for some collateral. Without that, our hands are tied."

The house was not paid for, but we had 50% paid, and we

used the home as collateral for part of the loan. So then the loan went through. In the next few months, we flew back to Germany with the money, and then we made the arrangements for how we print the boxes in German and in English, and we received the product later. It took a while to do that. In three or five months, we had the product ready, and they shipped it over to the States. This all happened in the '70s.

When we had the product over here, we had enough to get us to the Texas State Fair. Somebody was telling us where most people gather together: the Texas State Fair is the biggest, and then it's the Ohio State Fair. We figured we'd go to Texas. There were all kinds of people there with all different uses of metals. They have a lot of guns there, as well, and sporting goods. We showed them how it works on the guns, and how it was safe on factory gun bluing process. The fair went on for seventeen days.

At the Texas State Fair, we sold almost everything, and the last day we had hardly anything anymore, so we had a good start. We knew it was in the right direction. Then we wanted to work on the wholesale business, because everything now was retail direct sales.

We had translation sheets and reorder sheets in each tube that we sold. We had only tubes at that time. They were all in English, of course, but then we got some refilled retail orders from the customers at the Texas fair. They'd reorder by mail with checks, and then we sent them the orders. We sold out! We contacted each customer and told them it takes at least one to two months to get more Flitz. Anyway, people said, "Keep the checks, and when you get it, send us the Flitz." The checks were for about $10 to $20.

During the show in Texas, we had our biggest order from a gentleman by the name of Tom Phillips. He was a yacht captain for a large oil company. They had a big yacht in the Gulf. Tom Phillips was in charge of taking care of the yacht. He cleaned and maintained it so that everything runs right. He was at that show, and he bought some Flitz for the yacht. He liked it so much that he came back to the fair and told me that his boss in Fort Worth would like to talk to me. He wanted to have a meeting after the fair because he'd like to buy some Flitz. He will be in charge of the Flitz, besides taking care of the yacht, etc.

He gave me a business card, and after the show I called him and went down to his office. It was a tremendous office. It was really big with a lot of leather chairs, a first-class operation. At the meeting, there were three people. The oil company boss said they'd like to have the whole state of Texas. "Do you have distributors in Texas?" I said, "No, we don't have any distributors at all. We're just starting out." So he said they'd like to have Texas and maybe more, but to start out, that's good enough. Tom Phillips was the man in charge, and they would back him up with financing.

So then they came out with orders. They said they'd take some tubes. They'd like to have at least $30,000 worth of polish. That was just as much money as I had spent on developing the polish. I couldn't believe it! But then they said they'd give me half down and then we can order it, and when we're ready, we'll get it over to Texas via air shipment. I agreed, so we made the arrangements. They wrote me the check, 50% down (a check for $15,000). That was the biggest thrill that I had.

Then we came back to Wisconsin, and we ordered more of the Flitz. It was probably four weeks, and production was done for shipping in container by air via Lufthansa direct to Milwaukee, Wisconsin.

They called me from Texas and asked, "How fast we can get it?" I said, "Well, shipping by sea, it takes two, three weeks at least." He said, "Oh, that's too long. We've got to have it by air." I agreed and said, "Okay, we can have it shipped by air." So their shipment arrived by air. Lufthansa flew in that time direct from Germany to Milwaukee. There was a little bit for us, too, but most of it was for Texas. As the shipment arrived in Milwaukee, Uli's friend from Kentucky, John, was here on vacation to visit Uli. John came down to the airport and helped us unload it.

I called the Texas firm and said, "Your shipment is here. We'll get a truck shipment and forward it to you." They said, "No, that cannot be done. I told you air freight." And I said, "Yes, we have the air freight, but now it's in Milwaukee. You want air freight to Texas, as well?" He said, "Yes, we own Hugh Airlines. You bring it over to them in Milwaukee, and we'll call Hugh Airlines with the shipping papers."

So we shipped it to Texas via air with Hugh Airlines. They paid the air freight from Milwaukee to Ft. Worth, Texas. They received the product in good order. The Texas State Fair was the test ground for Flitz. It was my biggest single order. Texas has a special spot in my heart.

Time went on, and we worked other shows around the country and were very successful. We went to home shows, sport shows, boat shows, snowmobile shows, and motorcycle shows. Whatever we could get lined up, we did. In the beginning, we were away from home six months out of the year. We have seen the U.S. from the East Coast to the West Coast.

An early staff picture outside the FLITZ building.
Far left: Peter and Sieglinde.

In 1976, Uli came out of school. He liked selling and marketing, and so I said, "Would you like to come with me?" He agreed and said he'd like that. I said, "Okay, you come with me, and we will build the company together."

Then finally, it was maybe a year or not quite a year later

that the oil company boss called me. I don't know his name anymore. He said, "Do you know where Tom Phillips is?" I said, "No, I don't know. You should know, it's your man." He said, "Well, we thought that you would know. He's not there, and we cannot get ahold of him, and he owes us money."

Anyway, we never heard from the oil boss or Tom Phillips. We never got an order again. Tom's boss only told me, "If you don't know where he is, we will find him," and that was it. Evidently, they found Tom, and Tom paid everything back to them. But probably the trust was not there anymore with the oil company and him.

I was once at a sport show in Milwaukee, and a gentleman came by and asked me if I know Tom Phillips. And I said, "Yeah, I know Tom Phillips. We sold him Flitz through the oil company, and they backed him up." He said, "Yeah, that's my brother." It turned out he was the brother of Tom Phillips and lived in Lake Geneva. He was the inventor of the Weed Eaters. He mentioned to me, "When you deal with Tom again, don't trust him with money so much. Tom cannot manage money so good. I'd just like to tell you, my brother, he's otherwise a good man."

We still have customers in Texas. And of course, we sell a lot of wholesale. The first reps we had were in Chicago at the International Boat Show for wholesale. They called it the NAM show. We had some reps contact us to see if we'd like to work with them.

We said, "Yes, we look for reps." Then we had the first rep set up in Florida in the marine market. He lived in Florida.

He also had the Carolina states. That was his territory. He was a very good man. He did a good job for us, and he was with us until he passed away. He was a former marine. Then, of course, he steered us to other rep groups on the East Coast, more toward the Boston area. All of the reps, they knew each other, so we got more reps through him in the marine markets.

After a while, we got more into the wholesale shows. The trade shows, of course, they were marine, janitorial supply, sports and kitchen show markets, wholesale, and retail shows. Everything went good.

Eventually, we decided to produce the product here because shipping from Europe is expensive and time-consuming. We make the product over here, including all the packaging material, etc. The chemicals we got from Europe, but filling we never did. We shopped that out to a company in Chicago. They filled sample pouches, tubes, and cans of Flitz, and they mixed it to the specifications we needed. They did that for at least ten or fifteen years. Harold was the owner of the Paket Corporation, but then he passed away.

Somebody else bought his business after Harold passed on, so then we started with them. The new owner was not as good as Harold, so we found a company here in Wisconsin. That was probably five years ago (around 2015). The company is located in Germantown. It's a smaller company, and they still do our filling today.

Earlier this year (2021), we had tragic news fall upon us as we learned that the company owner at Packaging Sales, Inc. was killed in a UTV accident suddenly. His company, originally in

Germantown, had moved to Hartford and as before, had been Flitz products exclusively for years. Otto and Kathy Abolins were not only the owners, but we also became friends and business partners. Packaging Sales' legacy lives on, as we acquired the manufacturing side of his business and all of his machinery and employees. We are back to one family, under one roof and happy to know that his efforts live on in Flitz International's expansion in the manufacturing side of business!

We still lived in Sturtevant at our house and office we had there, but then we needed more room because the business grew so rapidly. There were a lot of children in the neighborhood, and UPS came every day to pick up product. We figured, well, that cannot last long because we are in a neighborhood which is not registered for commercial. There were a lot of deliveries, and we figured with the kids in the neighborhood, maybe something bad might happen.

So we looked for an industrial park in Racine with about an acre or more, and we found one in Waterford. It was, at that time, more reasonable than Racine. We moved to Waterford and built our first building. For two years, we drove every day from Sturtevant to Waterford.

After a while, our daughter, Angie, was done with college. Because she learned business administration, we needed her help and hired her right away. Linda had done all of the work so far, but it was too much for her. She couldn't handle it anymore, so we got Angie.

I hired Angie on a canoe trip over a weekend. She had several openings where they wanted to hire her as a business administration teacher. She could go to work at a high school teaching or something like that. But then I said, "Well, what do they offer you?" She told me what kind of money they would pay her, and I said, "We will pay you more if you come with us." She decided that day in the canoe to start with us. The money was better by us, so then she and Linda did the office.

Time goes on, and we got bigger and bigger. We hired more people. And of course, now we have a total of fifteen employees. Uli became the president when I retired from my post, and Linda retired as well. Then Angie took over as vice president of the company. My son, Olaf, is also in sales and customer relations. He has very good product knowledge, is very much liked by commercial customers, and is active with shows. The rest of the employees are not family related but are very loyal and very good people. Most of them stayed on with us a long time. Wilma just retired after twenty years.

My daughter, Silke, became a registered nurse. After college, she worked in a lot of hospitals. She liked her profession. During summer vacation while in college, she helped us out at boat shows in New Orleans to make extra pocket money. After the nursing career, she became a representative in the pharmaceutical industry for a company in Chicago. Her husband, Lloyd, worked in the same industry but for a different company. After she and her husband retired, she helped at the Flitz show promotion as an independent employee.

Flitz is still a successful business today – with thanks, to our loyal customers!

Pictured from left to right: Peter Kurt Jentzsch (May 6, 1935 – November 23, 2021), his wife Sieglinde Jentzsch (August 23, 1938 – October 2, 2012), and company mascot Flitzi!

Note from the Author

The greatest of pleasures and accomplishments noted in this book is the love of my family, to which I attribute my successes. From the days in East Germany to building our Flitz company here in the United States, my wife was an unwavering support and stronghold of our family. Her efforts combined with mine, and the love of family and friends, is what brought this story full circle. As we turn the pages to future chapters, our company remains in family hands with family ties . . . And the story continues.

About the Author
Peter Kurt Jentzsch (May 6, 1935 – November 23, 2021)

A quiet man of great thought, foresight, and graciousness is what made Peter Jentzsch special. Loved by many and discouraged by few, he made his way from East Germany to West Germany and eventually to the United States to live out the adventure of the American Dream while never forgetting his beloved homeland. Peter experienced a full life, not without struggle, but always with the support and love of his wife and children. He loved people, nature, and a challenge. Peter was a storyteller, and countless hours were taken to dictate, transcribe, and edit this work. A close friend helped in this quest after he was told by many that he should write a book . . . so here we have it! His hope was that this work be a human interest story not only to his own family but anyone who wanted to travel via his compass and witness the adventure he would term . . . As far as the East is from the West. May you all enjoy reading the story as much as he enjoyed telling it!